Pump up the volume of your holiday décor with plush pom-poms, tassels, fringe, and other simple crafts made from colorful yarn!

LEISURE ARTS, INC. • Maumelle, Arkansas

stitched cards

gather your stuff:

- 12" x $5^{1}/_{2}$" piece of cardstock for card
- glittered cardstock scrap
- medium weight yarn
- large-eye sharp needle
- star punch (about $^{1}/_{2}$" across)
- removable tape or painter's tape
- tracing paper
- craft glue
- old magazine

let's get started:

1. Crease and fold the cardstock into thirds *(Fig. 1)*.

2. Trace the desired pattern (page 24) onto tracing paper. Tape the pattern to the center panel of the unfolded card. Place the card on the old magazine and use the needle to punch holes through the center panel of the card *(Fig. 2)*.

3. Thread the needle with a 36" length of yarn. Backstitch *(Fig. 3)* the outline of the design, catching the yarn end under a few of the stitches. Once the outline is complete, fill in the design by stitching across the shape and going from one side to the other. Use additional yarn strands as needed. End the yarn by running it under a few stitches.

4. Fold the left card panel over the wrong side of the center panel stitching and glue in place. Punch stars from glittered cardstock and glue to card front.

Fig. 1

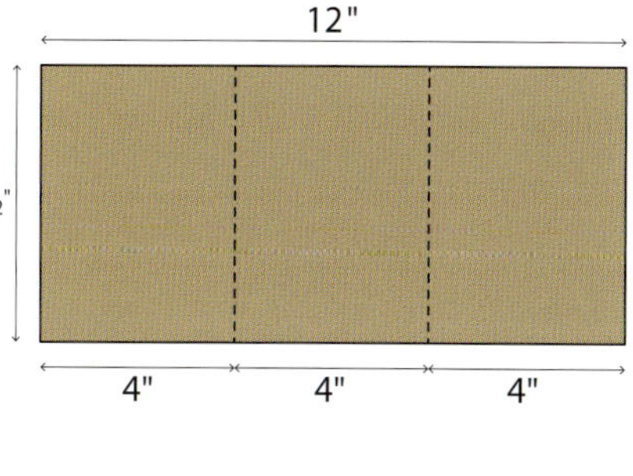

Fig. 2

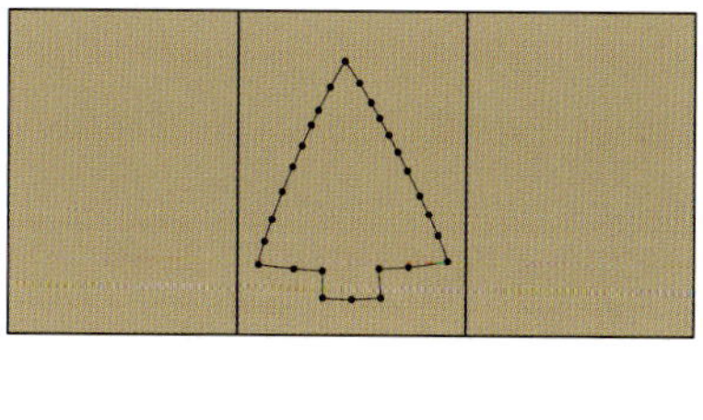

Fig. 3

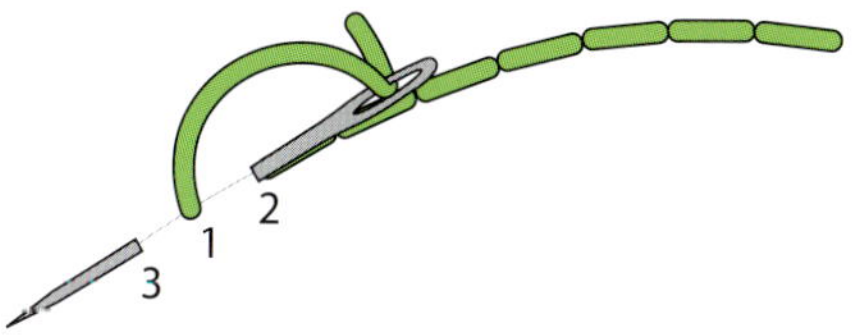

wreath

gather your stuff:

- pom-pom makers to make pom-poms that measure approximately $3^{3}/_{8}$", $2^{1}/_{2}$", & $1^{5}/_{8}$" in diameter
- five coordinating red & green yarn colors (each very large pom-pom: approximately 67 yards; each large pom-pom: approximately 39 yards; each medium pom-pom: approximately 15 yards)
- 20" square of foam core board
- craft knife
- hot glue gun & glue sticks

let's get started:

1. Cut an 18" diameter circle from the foam core board. Cut an 11" diameter circle from the center of the 18" circle.
2. Follow the manufacturer's instructions to make pom-poms in the desired sizes and colors. We made nine very large pom-poms, ten large pom-poms, and 29 medium pom-poms, for a total of 48 pom-poms.
3. Arrange the pom-poms as desired on the foam core circle. Glue in place.

light covers

gather your stuff:

- cotton yarn – 5 yards per light cover
- 4" balloons – one for each light cover
- strand of lights (we used a 20 light strand)
- liquid starch
- wax paper
- zipper-style resealable plastic bag

let's get started:

1. Blow up a balloon for each light, being careful to only blow the balloon into a round shape. Cover the work surface with wax paper.
2. Pour some starch into the plastic bag. Place a 5 yard length of yarn in the bag and seal. Knead and squish the yarn around in the bag until it is completely saturated with starch.
3. Carefully pull the yarn length from the plastic bag, squeezing out the excess starch as you remove the yarn; wrap the yarn around the balloon, criss-crossing the yarn several times over itself. Place the wrapped balloon on waxed paper to dry and harden. Make as many light covers as needed.
4. Once the light covers have dried and hardened, pop the balloons and discard. Use a small piece of matching yarn to tie each cover to the light strand.

pom-pom garland

gather your stuff:

- pom-pom maker to make pom-poms that measure approximately 2 1/2" in diameter
- seven coordinating colors of medium weight yarn - approximately 39 yards per pom-pom
- 2 130" lengths of bulky weight yarn for hanger
- large-eye yarn needle

let's get started:

1. Follow the manufacturer's instructions to make pom-poms. We made five of each color yarn.
2. Thread the needle with the 130" yarn lengths. Thread the pom-poms on the yarn lengths, placing the colors as desired.

{ Follow Finger Crochet instructions, page 22, to make coordinating yarn chain garlands. }

tree plaque

gather your stuff:

- 5" x 7" wood plaque
- green/white variegated medium weight yarn – about 15 yards
- 18" length of floral wire
- $^{1}/_{2}$" diameter gold sparkle pom-pom
- 6mm assorted color pom-poms for ornaments
- white spray paint
- clear acrylic spray sealer
- liquid starch
- 8" x 10" gold frame with backing board
- wire cutters
- hot glue gun & glue sticks

let's get started:

1. Spray the plaque white, being sure to paint the sides. Allow to dry thoroughly. Spray with acrylic sealer and allow to dry.

2. Cut a 6" length of floral wire. Cut 58 8" lengths of yarn. Starting about $1^{1}/_{4}$" from one wire end, tie the yarn lengths around the wire length. Run a very thin line of glue over the knots on the wrong side of the tree. Wrap the exposed wire end with yarn, gluing as necessary.

3. Pour the liquid starch in a shallow dish. Dip the tree into the starch and let the yarn become saturated. Squeeze out the excess starch. Place the tree on the plaque, bending the wire to create a slightly curved tree. Use your finger to gently pull out the tree "branches", smoothing and coaxing them into place. Trim the yarn ends as desired to create the tree shape.

4. Allow the starch to dry. Glue any sections of the tree that are not adhered to the plaque. Glue the sparkle pom-pom to the tree top and the 6mm pom-poms to the tree for ornaments.

5. Remove and discard frame glass. Remove the backing board from the frame and spray white; allow to dry. Replace the board in the frame and glue the tree plaque to the center.

wall hanging

gather your stuff:

- tree branch (ours is approximately 36" long)
- dark red & red super bulky weight yarn - approximately 80 yards each
- gold super bulky weight yarn - approximately 40 yards
- white spray paint

let's get started:

1. Spray the tree branch white. Allow to dry completely.
2. Cut 60 45" lengths of the dark red yarn, 60 45" lengths of the red yarn, and 30 45" lengths of the gold yarn. Holding ten strands of yarn together, tie the yarn lengths in lark's head knots around the tree branch *(Fig. 1)* in the following order: dark red, red, dark red, red, dark red, red, 3 sets of gold, red, dark red, red, dark red, red, dark red.

Fig. 1

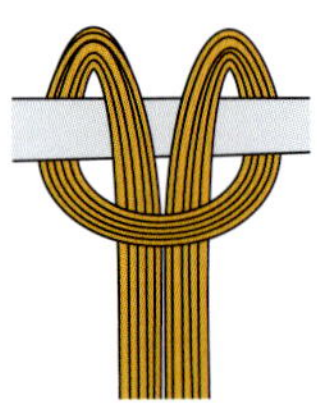

3. Trim the yarn ends to a pointed chevron.

trees

gather your stuff:

- foam cones (we used 6", 9" & 12" tall cones)
- medium weight or bulky weight variegated or solid color yarn
- pom-pom maker to make a pom-pom that measures approximately 1⁵/₈" in diameter
- hot glue gun & glue sticks

let's get started:

1. For each tree, wrap the yarn around a foam cone, securing the ends with glue.
2. Follow the manufacturer's instructions to make a pom-pom. Glue the pom-pom to the cone top.

joy

gather your stuff:

- J, O, Y papier-mache letters, about 8 1/2" tall
- red variegated bulky weight yarn
- low-temp glue gun & glue sticks

let's get started:

1. For the tops of the J and Y, glue the ends of short yarn lengths across the letter tops and the end of the J.
2. Keeping the yarn as straight as possible, wrap the J and O with yarn, securing the ends with glue.
3. On the Y, start at the base and wrap the center leg up to the split. Wrap each upper arm separately.

star ornaments

gather your stuff:

- 3 1/4" plastic canvas star shape – 2 for each ornament
- medium weight metallic yarn
- #16 tapestry needle
- cotton balls

let's get started:

1. For each ornament, follow the chart below to stitch 2 stars (see Stitch Diagrams, page 23). Use overcast stitches to join the stars together along the outer edges, placing a few cotton balls between the stars just before stitching the final stitches.

2. For the hanging loop, cut a 5" length of yarn. Thread the yarn through the ornament and knot the ends together.

Ornament (stitch 2)

snowman

gather your stuff:

- white medium weight yarn
- 12" of 5/8" wide ribbon
- 2 small red pom-poms
- red chenille stem
- pom-poms or buttons for facial features & front buttons
- pom-pom makers to make pom-poms that measure approximately 2 1/2" & 3 3/8" in diameter
- hot glue gun & glue sticks

let's get started:

1. Follow the manufacturer's instructions to make two white pom-poms, one in each size. Stack and tie the pom-poms together, adding glue if necessary.

2. For the ear muffs, cut a 7" length of the red chenille stem. Twist each end into a small circle. Glue the red pom-poms over the circle ends. Glue the ear muffs to the snowman.

3. Tie the ribbon around the snowman's neck; trim the ends. Glue the pom-poms or buttons to the snowman for the facial features and front buttons.

fringed garland

gather your stuff:

- thin jute rope for base
- three coordinating colors of bulky weight yarn (we used metallic gold, metallic silver, & cream yarns, 85-100 yards of each color)

let's get started:

1. Cut the desired length of jute for the base, plus 12" (we cut a 120" length). Tie a knot at each end.
2. Cut a 25" length of yarn for fringe. Refer to Fig. 1 and use a lark's head knot to tie the fringe to the base near one end.

Fig. 1

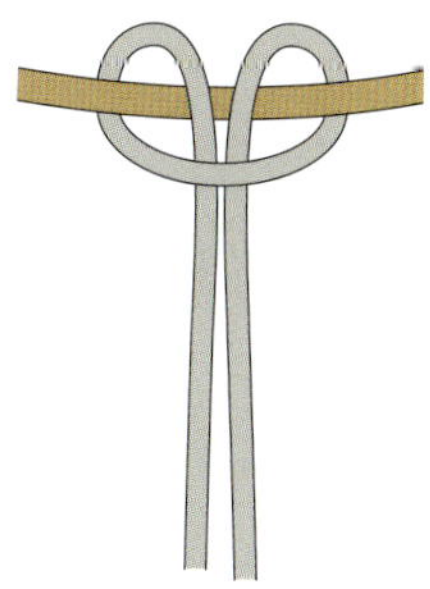

3. Continue to add fringe lengths to the base until the base is as full as you'd like. We used groups of 10 cream yarn lengths and groups of 20 silver or gold yarn lengths. Trim the fringe as desired.

tasseled throw

gather your stuff:

- throw or small blanket
- six coordinating colors of bulky weight yarn (approximately 7 yards for each tassel)
- 5" x 3" piece of sturdy mat board or cardboard
- hand sewing needle
- sewing thread to coordinate with throw & yarns

{ Make longer and fuller tassels to sew on the corners of a simple pillow. }

let's get started:

Referring to instructions below, make as many tassels as desired for the throw. Hand sew the tassels to the throw (we sewed 18 tassels on opposite ends, spacing them about $2^{1}/_{2}$" to 3" apart).

Making a Tassel

1. Wrap yarn around the mat board 22 times. Trim the yarn from the skein. Slip a 10" length of yarn behind the wraps and bring it to the top of the mat board; tie a secure knot. Cut the yarn loops on the end opposite the knot *(Fig. 1)*.
2. Remove the mat board. Holding the yarn ends together, tie a 10" yarn length around the tassel about $^{1}/_{2}$" below the knot *(Fig. 2)*. Trim all yarn ends.

Fig. 1

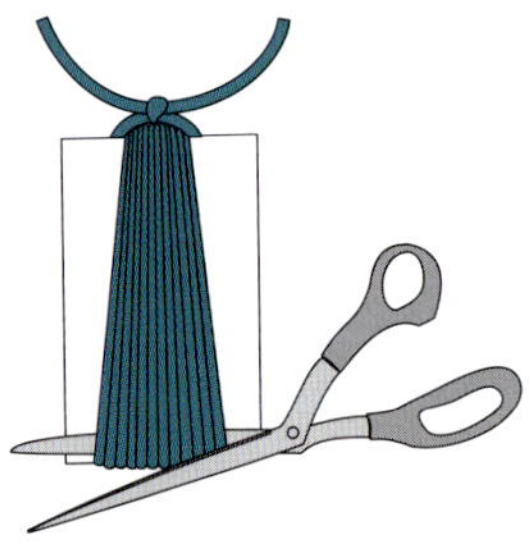

Fig. 2

hat ornaments

gather your stuff:

- paper towel or bathroom tissue cardboard tube
- 7 yards of medium weight yarn for each hat
- 12" length of thin metallic cord for each hanger

let's get started:

1. To make one hat, cut a 3/4" tall ring from the cardboard tube *(Fig. 1)*.

Fig. 1

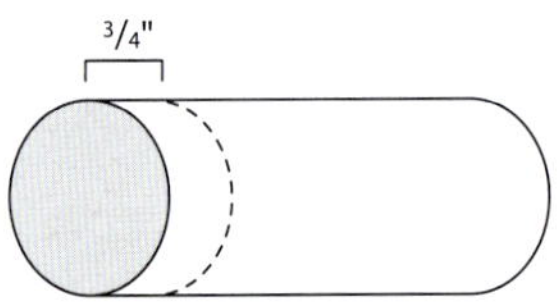

2. Cut 29 8" lengths of medium weight yarn. Tie each yarn length around the cardboard ring with a lark's head knot *(Fig. 2)*.

Fig. 2

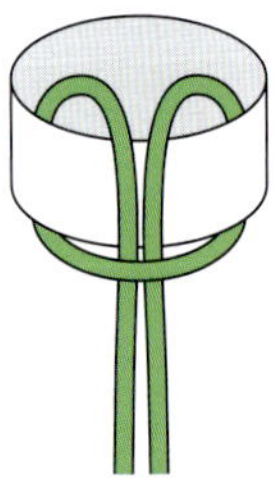

3. Pull all the yarn ends up through the ring center. Use a 12" yarn length to tie the ends together about 1" above the ring *(Fig. 3)*. Trim the hat yarn lengths to about 1/2" so that they resemble a pom-pom. Tie a metallic cord length to the top for the hanger.

Fig. 3

finger crochet

1. To start a finger crochet chain, make a slip knot about 4" from the yarn end by grabbing the yarn at the star and pulling it through the top loop *(Fig. 1)*; tighten the new loop you just made.

2. Grab the working yarn and pull it through the loop as indicated by the arrows *(Fig. 2)*, creating a chain stitch *(Fig. 3)*. Tighten the new loop.

3. Continue making new chain stitches until the chain is the desired length. Trim the yarn about 4" from the last chain stitch and pull the end through that stitch *(Fig. 4)* and tighten.

Fig. 1

Fig. 2

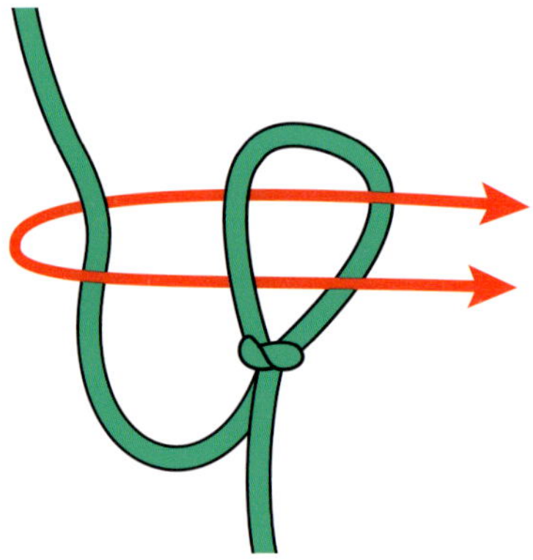

Fig. 3

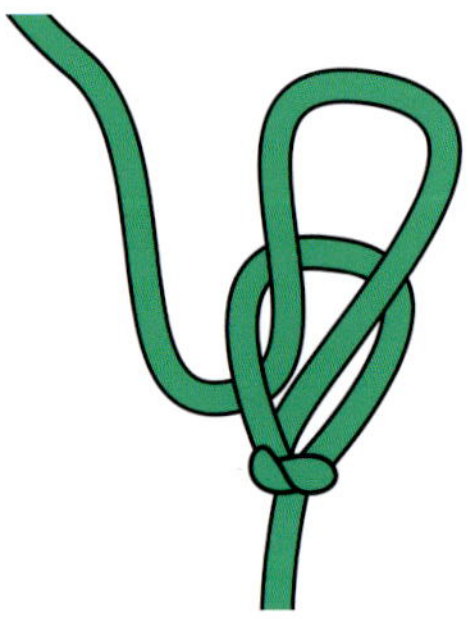

Fig. 4

stitch diagrams

*Unless otherwise indicated, bring the threaded needle up at **1** and all **odd** numbers and down **2** and all **even** numbers.*

Gobelin Stitch

This basic straight stitch is worked over two or more threads or intersections *(Fig. 5)*. The number of threads or intersections may vary according to the chart.

Fig. 5

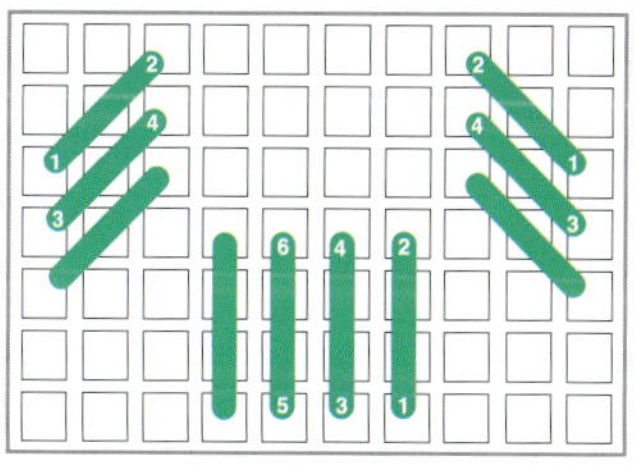

Overcast Stitch

This stitch covers the edge of the canvas *(Fig. 6)* and is used to join canvas pieces. It may be necessary to go through the same hole more than once to get even coverage on the edge, especially at the corners.

Fig. 6

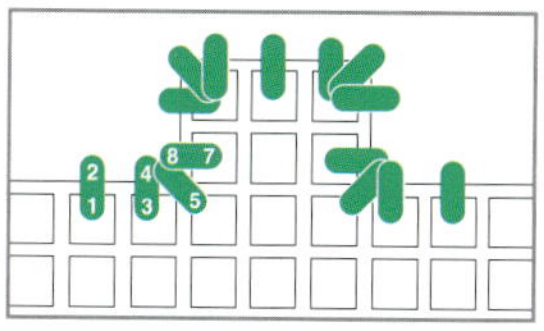

card patterns

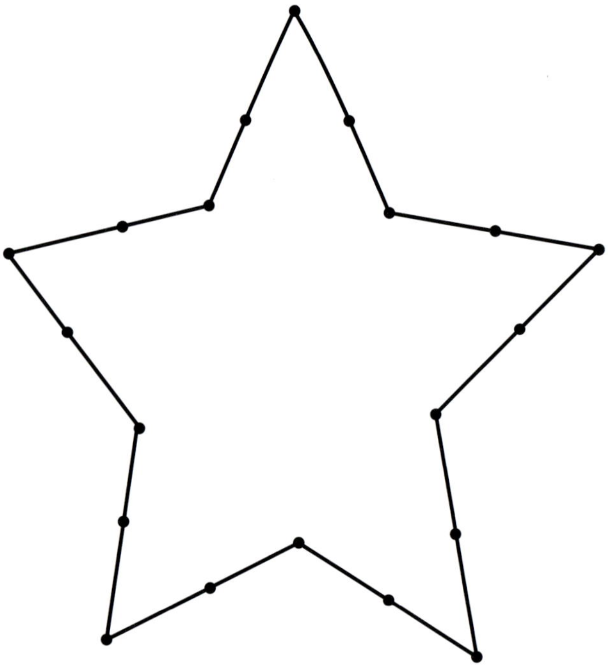

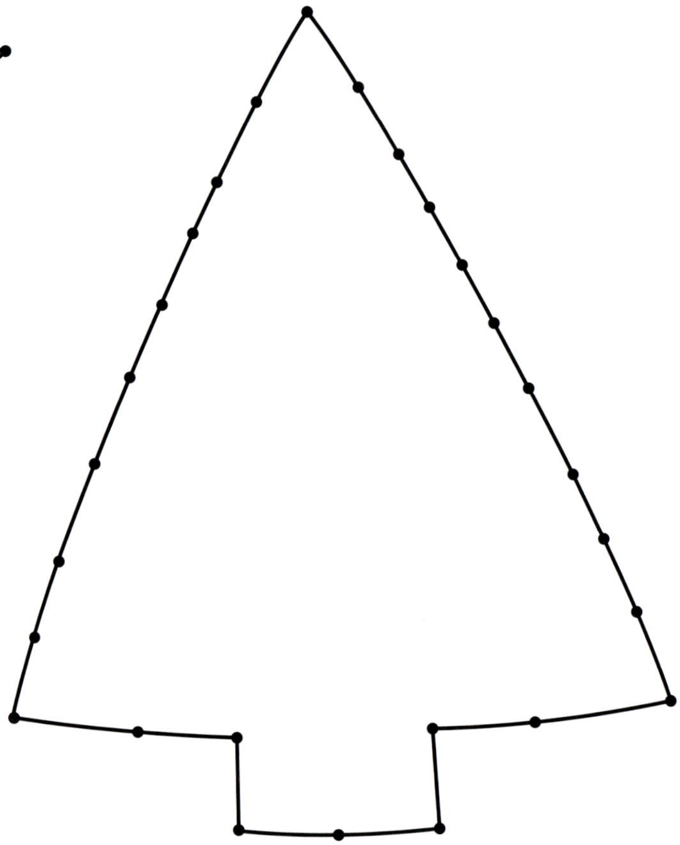

Production Team: Designer – Kelly Reider; Technical Writer – Mary Sullivan Hutcheson; Technical Associate – Lisa Lancaster; Editorial Writer – Susan Frantz Wiles; Senior Graphic Artist – Lora Puls; Associate Graphic Artist – Frances Huddleston; Photostylist – Lori Wenger; Photographer – Jason Masters.